REMARKABLE PEOPLE

Barack Obama

by Michael De Medeiros

MEDIA ENHANCED BOOKS

AV2 BY WEIGL

ADDED VALUE • AUDIO VISUAL

www.av2books.com

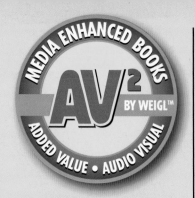

MEDIA ENHANCED BOOKS
AV²
BY WEIGL™
ADDED VALUE • AUDIO VISUAL

AV² provides enriched content that supplements and complements this book. Weigl's AV² books strive to create inspired learning and engage young minds in a total learning experience.

Your AV² Media Enhanced books come alive with...

Audio
Listen to sections of the book read aloud.

Key Words
Study vocabulary, and complete a matching word activity.

Go to **www.av2books.com**, and enter this book's unique code.

Video
Watch informative video clips.

Quizzes
Test your knowledge.

BOOK CODE

S 6 1 2 7 2 7

Embedded Weblinks
Gain additional information for research.

Slide Show
View images and captions, and prepare a presentation.

AV² by Weigl brings you media enhanced books that support active learning.

Try This!
Complete activities and hands-on experiments.

... and much, much more!

Published by AV² by Weigl
350 5th Avenue, 59th Floor
New York, NY 10118

www.av2books.com   www.weigl.com

Copyright ©2014 AV² by Weigl

Library of Congress Cataloging-in-Publication Data available upon request.
Fax 1-866-349-3445 for the attention of the Publishing Records department.

ISBN 978-1-62127-388-2 (hardcover)
ISBN 978-1-62127-394-3 (softcover)

Printed in the United States of America in North Mankato, Minnesota
1 2 3 4 5 6 7 8 9 0 17 16 15 14 13

WEP300113
032013

Editors: Megan Cuthbert and Heather Kissock
Design: Terry Paulhus

Photograph Credits
Weigl acknowledges Getty Images as the primary image supplier for this title. Every reasonable effort has been made to trace ownership and to obtain permission to reprint copyright material. The publishers would be pleased to have any errors or omissions brought to their attention so that they may be corrected in subsequent printings.

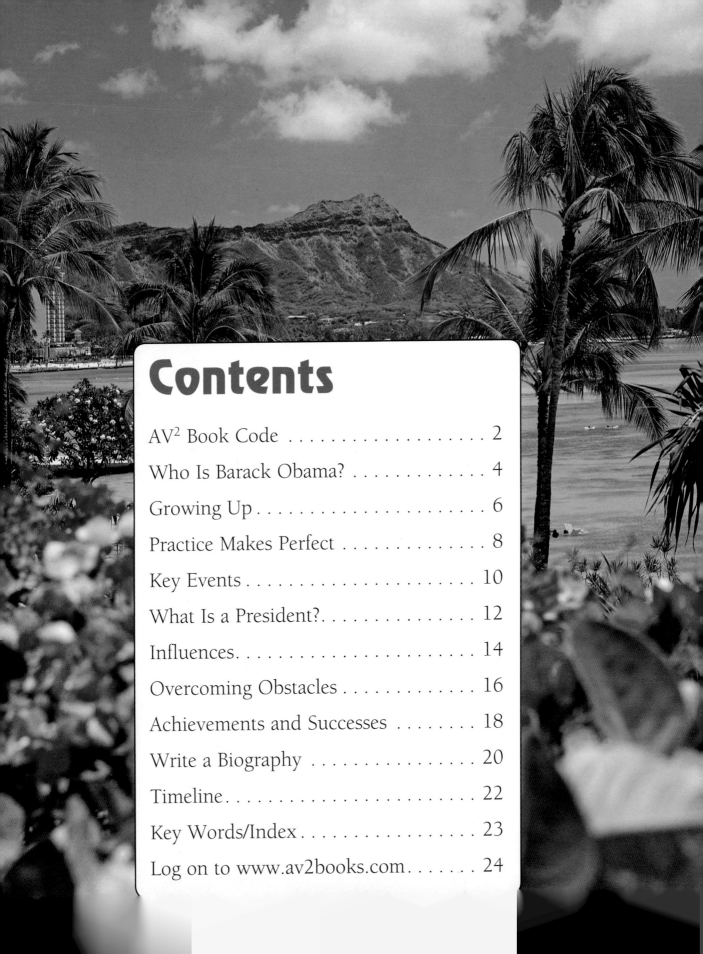

Contents

Who Is Barack Obama?

Barack Obama is America's 44th president. When he was inaugurated on January 20, 2009, Barack became the country's first African American president and the first president born in the state of Hawai'i. He was re-elected in 2012 and began his second term as president in January 2013.

Barack began his political career in 1997 as an Illinois state senator. Then, in 2004, Barack won a seat in the United States Senate. Three years later, Barack became the first African American chosen to run for president for a major U.S. political party. Barack's presidency began after he defeated the Republican nominee, John McCain, in the general election.

"With common effort and common purpose, with passion and dedication, let us answer the call of history, and carry into an uncertain future that precious light of freedom."

As president, Barack has guided the country through many challenges, from a poor economy to a debate about gun control. By working to solve these issues, Barack has helped to improve the quality of life for many Americans.

Barack Obama

Growing Up

Barack Hussein Obama II was born on August 4, 1961, in Honolulu, Hawai'i. Barack was named after his father. Barack Sr. was an African student studying economics at the University of Hawai'i. Barack's mother, Ann Dunham, was a student from Kansas attending the same university. When Barack was two years old, his parents separated. They later divorced. Barack and his mother stayed in Hawai'i. Barack Sr. went to study at Harvard University, in Massachusetts, before returning to Africa.

When Barack was six years old, his mother married Lolo Soetoro, an Indonesian foreign exchange student. Lolo, Ann, and Barack moved to Jakarta, Indonesia. At school in Jakarta, Barack was a good student and learned to speak Indonesian. However, his mother felt he could get a better education in the United States. In 1971, Barack returned to Honolulu to live with his grandparents and attend a private school. Barack's mother, stepfather, and half-sister, Maya, stayed in Jakarta. It was a lonely time for Barack. He missed his mother and sister. Though he grew close to his grandparents, he struggled with being one of the only African American students in his school.

■ In a third grade assignment, Barack wrote that he wanted to be president when he grew up.

Get to Know Hawai'i

FLOWER
Hibiscus

TREE
Kukui

BIRD
Nene

HAWAIIAN ISLANDS

Pacific Ocean

N
0   100 Miles
0   100 Kilometers

There are eight main Hawaiian Islands—Niihau, Kauai, Oahu, Molokai, Lanai, Kahoolawe, Maui, and Hawai'i—and hundreds of other islands.

More than one third of the world's pineapples come from Hawai'i.

Mauna Loa, a volcano on the island of Hawai'i, is the world's largest active volcano.

The capital city of Hawai'i is Honolulu. It is located on the island of Oahu.

Hawai'i became the 50th U.S. state on August 21, 1959. It is the only island state.

Think about it!

Barack moved to Jakarta, Indonesia in 1967. Imagine moving to the other side of the world. Make a chart comparing your home to another country. How are things like language, weather, food, clothing, jobs, or nature the same or different?

Practice Makes Perfect

Barack grew up in a family where **cultural diversity** and education were considered important. His parents were of different racial **ancestry**, and both his mother and father pursued advanced college degrees. Being surrounded by different cultures and a love of learning, Barack developed an interest in people and the world. He was always aware of conflicts in other countries and wanted to talk about them. To learn more about the world, Barack read on his own, especially books about politics, **philosophy**, and religion.

■ Living in Indonesia with his mother and stepfather allowed Barack to experience other cultures and ways of life at an early age.

When Barack finished high school, he studied at Occidental College in Los Angeles for two years before transferring to Columbia University, where he studied international relations. Barack learned about economics, political science, **sociology**, history, and business. After graduating from university, Barack went to Chicago to work as a community organizer. In this job, he worked with churches to improve conditions for people living in poor neighborhoods on Chicago's South Side.

QUICK FACTS

- In Swahili, Barack means "one who is blessed."

- Barack was the first African American president of the Harvard Law Review.

- Barack's wife, Michelle, is a lawyer. Michelle, like Barack, graduated from Harvard Law School.

However, Barack realized that to make a big difference in people's lives, he would have to change laws and politics. He enrolled at Harvard Law School. Barack graduated from law school **magna cum laude**. He returned to Chicago to work, teach, and practice law. A few years later, in 1996, Barack won a seat in the Illinois State Senate.

■ Barack met his wife Michelle in 1989, when they worked at the same law firm. They married in 1992 and now have two daughters, Sasha and Malia.

Key Events

Four months after giving an inspiring **keynote address** at the 2004 Democratic National Convention, Barack was elected to the United States Senate. He was only the third African American to sit in the Senate since **Reconstruction**.

In 2008, Barack was chosen as the Democratic candidate for president. Barack faced a tough race against his Republican rival, John McCain. After months of campaigning, Barack was elected as the first African American president of the United States. It was an important milestone for **civil rights** in the country. Barack's inauguration in January 2009 was attended by several prominent civil rights leaders and witnessed by a record crowd.

Barack was re-elected for a second term as president in 2012. His public inauguration on January 21, 2013 coincided with Martin Luther King, Jr. Day. This national holiday celebrates Martin Luther King, Jr., a civil rights leader who helped end **segregation** in the United States.

■ At his 2013 inauguration, Barack took his oath on Martin Luther King, Jr.'s Bible.

Thoughts from Barack

Barack has always had an interest in helping people. Here are some things he has said about his political beliefs and his life.

Barack tries to inspire people.

"If you're walking down the right path and you're willing to keep walking, eventually you'll make progress."

Barack explains his job as a politician.

"My job is not to represent Washington to you, but to represent you to Washington."

Barack explains the responsibilities of being an American citizen.

"The freedom which so many Americans have fought for and died for comes with responsibilities as well as rights, and among those are love and charity and duty and patriotism. That's what makes America great."

Barack wants people to strive to be their best.

"We need to internalize this idea of excellence. Not many folks spend a lot of time trying to be excellent."

Barack talks about the future.

"I believe we can provide jobs to the jobless, homes to the homeless, and reclaim young people in cities across America from violence and despair."

Barack talks about democracy.

"Democracy is not something that is static; it's something that we constantly have to work on."

What Is a President?

The president of the United States is the **head of state** and head of the government, as well as commander-in-chief of the armed forces. As commander-in-chief, the president has the power to send troops to combat. As the head of state and government, the president enforces laws and creates policies. The president is also responsible for preparing the **federal budget** and appointing officials. He or she does not have the power to make these decisions alone. The president must work with Congress to complete these tasks. Together, they make decisions on behalf of the American people.

The president is usually elected to the position. To run for the presidency, a person must be at least 35 years old and be a natural born citizen of the United States. A candidate also must prove that he or she has lived in the United States for at least 14 years. A president serves a term of four years. If re-elected, a president may serve an additional four-year term. A person can serve as president for no more than two terms.

■ The president is responsible for giving an annual State of the Union address before Congress. This address outlines the condition of the country and any new laws the president plans to introduce.

Presidents 101

George Washington (1732–1799)

George Washington was the first president of the United States. George had served as general and commander-in-chief of the colonial armies during the American Revolution. He was the first leader in history to successfully win a revolution over a colonial power. After being elected as president, George became the first person to take the oath of office, on April 30, 1789. George Washington served two terms as president and played a crucial role in molding the country.

Abraham Lincoln (1809–1865)

Abraham Lincoln was inaugurated as the country's 16th president in 1861. He fought to keep the country together during the Civil War. In 1863, he issued the Emancipation Proclamation, freeing slaves in several states. When Abraham was re-elected as president, African Americans participated in the inaugural parade for the first time. In 1865, Abraham Lincoln was the first president to be assassinated.

Franklin D. Roosevelt (1882–1945)

Franklin D. Roosevelt was elected president in 1932. Franklin's policies helped guide the American people through the Great Depression. In 1933, Franklin became the first president to appoint a woman to his **cabinet**. He was a popular leader and was elected to four terms as president. He was the first and last president to serve more than two terms in office. Franklin died in 1945, shortly after beginning his fourth term.

John F. Kennedy (1917–1963)

John F. Kennedy became the country's 35th president in 1961. He was the youngest person ever elected president, and also the first Roman Catholic in the role. John was a charismatic leader and speaker. During his brief time as president, he championed civil rights and managed to avoid nuclear war with Russia. In November 1963, John F. Kennedy was assassinated. He was the youngest president to die.

Politicians

Politicians are the people who run federal, state, and local governments. Their job is to make and pass laws for the people of the area or country they represent. In a democracy, politicians are elected by the people of a place. To make sure the people are being represented, the United States holds elections every two to four years. If people are not satisfied with what their politicians are doing for them, they have the chance to choose someone new during an election.

Influences

When Barack was 10 years old, his father visited him in Hawai'i. Barack had not seen his father since he was two years old and did not remember him. During the visit, Barack's father spoke about life in Africa, specifically about **tribal customs** and Kenya's opposition to British rule. Barack remembers his father telling him about Kenya's struggle to be free. Barack's father talked about how many people had been enslaved because of the color of their skin. He told Barack how Kenyans longed to be free and develop themselves through hard work and sacrifice, just as African Americans had done in the United States following the Civil War.

Barack learned a valuable lesson from his father. The message of people sharing common goals across race, geography, and history helped shape the way Barack saw the world. Barack's father went back to Kenya, and Barack never saw him again. Barack Sr. died in a car accident in 1982.

■ Barack wrote a book, called *Dreams from My Father*, to reflect on the experiences he had growing up without his father.

Barack's interest in politics grew after the visit with his father. He began to watch and listen to politicians in the United States and around the world. Barack was inspired by many great leaders of the past. Some of his political heroes include Martin Luther King, Jr., Congressman John Lewis, Mahatma Gandhi, and President Abraham Lincoln. Barack believes these leaders gave hope and a sense of purpose to people. He tries to do the same.

DR. LAURENCE TRIBE

Dr. Laurence Tribe is one of America's leading teachers and **scholars** in **constitutional** law. He is a professor of law at Harvard University, one of the most respected universities in the world. Laurence was one of Barack's professors, and a **mentor** to Barack, when he studied at Harvard. Laurence helped shape the way Barack thought about civil rights, the Constitution, and the law. Laurence says Barack was "one of the two most talented students I've had in 37 years of teaching. When I look at my kids and grandkids and ask what makes me hopeful about the future—one thing is Barack Obama."

■ During his years at Harvard Law School, Barack worked as a research assistant for Laurence Tribe.

Overcoming Obstacles

Being the child of mixed-race parents was often a challenge for Barack. Living with his aging grandparents and away from his father and mother, Barack found it difficult to grow up without a father or African American role model. It was not until he left Hawai'i to attend college that his life began to find focus. He started to redefine what it meant to him to be a strong African American.

Throughout his life and work, Barack has dealt with racism. He struggles to get people to see him for the work he does instead of the color of his skin. Sometimes, racism can be dangerous. When Barack announced he wanted to run for president, some people in the United States became angry and threatened to harm Barack. Barack now has a large group of Secret Service bodyguards to protect him everywhere he goes.

■ Barack's grandparents were a major influence in his life. He lived with them until he finished high school in 1979.

When Barack was elected, the country was facing a financial crisis. Many companies were going **bankrupt**. People were losing their jobs, which left them unable to pay their bills. Americans were worried about their future. To try to keep businesses open, Barack and his government provided loans to several large companies. The businesses stayed open, so people were able to keep their jobs and pay their bills. Slowly, businesses began to start making money again, and Americans started to feel more secure.

Barack decided to make gun control a key issue for his second term as president. He believes that changing the laws about gun ownership will help keep Americans safe. In January 2013, Barack signed several **executive orders** on gun control and asked Congress to pass laws that help protect American citizens against gun violence.

■ The financial crisis of the mid-2000s was felt across the country. Some people lost their homes because they could not afford to make their house payments to the bank.

Achievements and Successes

In 1995, Barack published his autobiography, or life story. The book, called *Dreams from My Father*, told the story of his childhood and youth. *Dreams from My Father* became a bestseller. The audio version of the book won a Grammy Award for Best Spoken Word Album in 2006.

Barack published his second book, *The Audacity of Hope*, in 2006. It reached the top of the *New York Times* Best Sellers list. In the months between winning the 2008 election and taking office, Barack wrote his third book, *Of Thee I Sing: A Letter to My Daughters*. The book is an illustrated letter to Barack's two daughters, Malia and Sasha. It tells the stories of 13 influential Americans and how their actions continue to affect new generations.

■ Barack visited schools and libraries to read sections from *Of Thee I Sing: A Letter to My Daughters* to children.

When Barack took office, one of his first tasks as president was changing the health care laws. He wanted to make health care more affordable and available to all Americans. Following a long series of debates, Barack and his government passed the Patient Protection and Affordable Care Act and reformed the country's health care system.

During the second year of his presidency, Barack and his government were able to locate Osama bin Laden, the terrorist who planned the September 11, 2001 attacks on New York City. For many years, the American government had been trying to find Osama bin Laden. It was considered a major triumph for Barack that the world's most wanted man was discovered during his presidency.

THE NOBEL PRIZE

Just nine months into his presidency, Barack was awarded the Nobel Peace Prize. This prize is given to people who have made a major contribution toward attaining world peace. The Nobel committee gave the prize to Barack because of his attempts to improve relations between countries. He was also praised for his attempts to stop the spread of nuclear weapons. Barack donated the prize money, about $1.4 million, to charity. He is the third U.S. president to receive the award while still in office. Theodore Roosevelt and Woodrow Wilson also won while president. Jimmy Carter was awarded the prize after he had left office.

Write a Biography

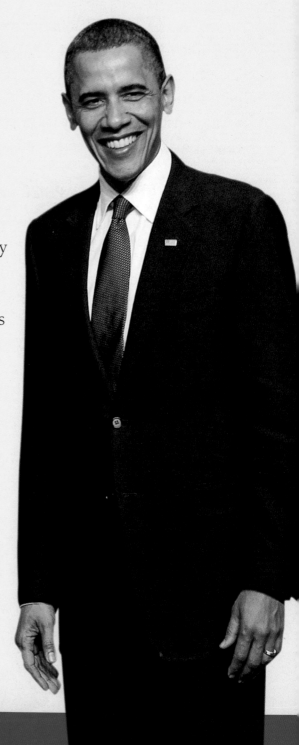

A person's life story can be the subject of a book. This kind of book is called a biography. Biographies describe the lives of remarkable people, such as those who have achieved great success or have done important things to help others. These people may be alive today, or they may have lived many years ago. Reading a biography can help you learn more about a remarkable person.

At school, you might be asked to write a biography. First, decide who you want to write about. You can choose a political figure, such as Barack Obama, or any other person. Then, find out if your library has any books about this person. Learn as much as you can about him or her. Write down the key events in this person's life. What was this person's childhood like? What has he or she accomplished? What are his or her goals? What makes this person special or unusual?

A concept web is a useful research tool. Read the questions in the following concept web. Answer the questions in your notebook. Your answers will help you write a biography.

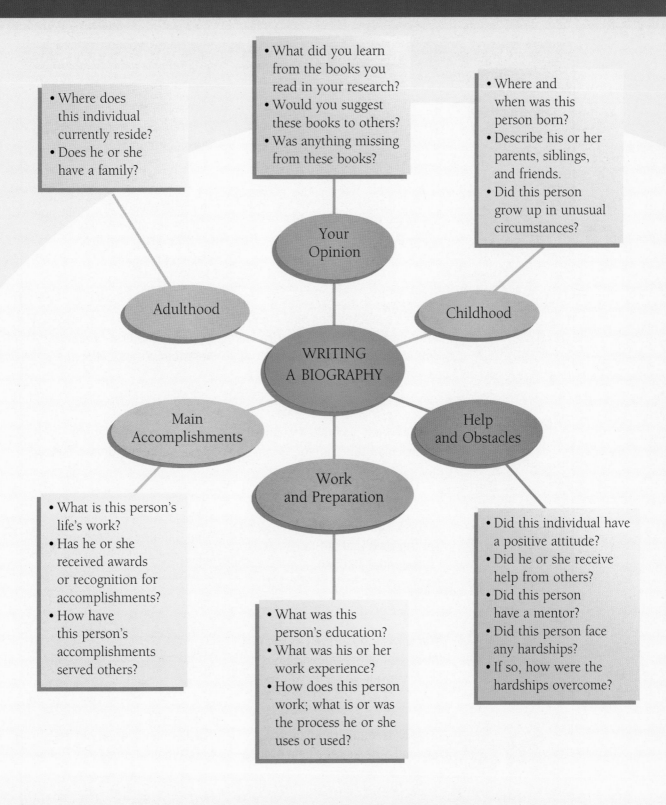

- Where does this individual currently reside?
- Does he or she have a family?

- What did you learn from the books you read in your research?
- Would you suggest these books to others?
- Was anything missing from these books?

- Where and when was this person born?
- Describe his or her parents, siblings, and friends.
- Did this person grow up in unusual circumstances?

Your Opinion

Adulthood

Childhood

WRITING A BIOGRAPHY

Main Accomplishments

Help and Obstacles

Work and Preparation

- What is this person's life's work?
- Has he or she received awards or recognition for accomplishments?
- How have this person's accomplishments served others?

- What was this person's education?
- What was his or her work experience?
- How does this person work; what is or was the process he or she uses or used?

- Did this individual have a positive attitude?
- Did he or she receive help from others?
- Did this person have a mentor?
- Did this person face any hardships?
- If so, how were the hardships overcome?

Timeline

YEAR	BARACK OBAMA	WORLD EVENTS
1961	Barack is born on August 4 in Honolulu, Hawai'i.	The Berlin Wall is built to separate East Germany and West Germany.
1982	Barack's father dies in a car accident.	The Falklands War begins because Argentina invades Great Britain's Falkland Islands.
1995	Barack's mother dies only months after his bestselling book, *Dreams from My Father*, is published.	Dr. Bernard A. Harris, Jr. becomes the first African American to walk in space.
1996	Barack wins his first election to the Illinois State Senate.	Bill Clinton is re-elected president of the United States.
2007	Barack announces his candidacy for the 2008 United States presidential election.	Nancy Pelosi, a Democrat from California, becomes Congress' first female speaker of the house.
2009	Barack is inaugurated as the 44th president of the United States.	Jóhanna Sigurðardóttir is elected as the first female prime minister of Iceland.
2013	Barack is inaugurated for his second term as president of the United States.	The 60th anniversary of the coronation of England's Queen Elizabeth II takes place.

Key Words

ancestry: the people in a family who lived several generations ago

bankrupt: not able to pay what one owes

cabinet: a group of people appointed by the president to head the executive departments of the government

civil rights: the rights given by a nation's government to all its citizens

constitutional: concerning the system of rights and laws by which a nation or state is governed

cultural diversity: of different racial, ethnic, or religious backgrounds

democracy: a form of government in which the power lies with the people

executive orders: orders issued by the president that have the force of law

federal budget: the overall financial plan for a country

head of state: the chief representative of a country

keynote address: a speech that presents the main ideas of interest to the audience

magna cum laude: the second-highest honor given upon graduation from university

mentor: someone who guides another person

philosophy: the study of life, truth, knowledge, and other important human matters

Reconstruction: the period in U.S. history following the Civil War and the end of slavery

scholars: people who have a great deal of knowledge, usually acquired from research and study

segregation: the enforced separation of people based on race

sociology: the study of human societies

tribal customs: the traditional practices and characteristics of a tribe or tribes

Index

Log on to www.av2books.com

AV² by Weigl brings you media enhanced books that support active learning. Go to www.av2books.com, and enter the special code found on page 2 of this book. You will gain access to enriched and enhanced content that supplements and complements this book. Content includes video, audio, weblinks, quizzes, a slide show, and activities.

AV² Online Navigation

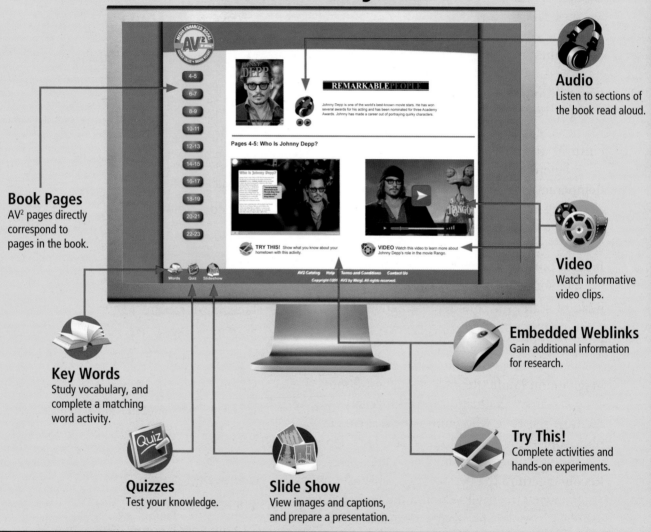

Audio
Listen to sections of the book read aloud.

Book Pages
AV² pages directly correspond to pages in the book.

Video
Watch informative video clips.

Key Words
Study vocabulary, and complete a matching word activity.

Embedded Weblinks
Gain additional information for research.

Quizzes
Test your knowledge.

Slide Show
View images and captions, and prepare a presentation.

Try This!
Complete activities and hands-on experiments.

AV² was built to bridge the gap between print and digital. We encourage you to tell us what you like and what you want to see in the future.

Sign up to be an AV² Ambassador at www.av2books.com/ambassador.